PACIFIC COAST HORNS
VOLUME 2

BLOW YOUR OWN HORN

FRENCH HORN

MUSIC MINUS ONE

3555

SUGGESTIONS FOR USING THIS MMO EDITION

WE HAVE TRIED to create a product that will provide you an easy way to learn and perform these compositions with a full ensemble in the comfort of your own home. The following MMO features and techniques will help you maximize the effectiveness of the MMO practice and performance system:

Because it involves a fixed accompaniment performance, there is an inherent lack of flexibility in tempo. We have observed generally accepted tempi, and always in the originally intended key, but some may wish to perform at a different tempo, or to slow down or speed up the accompaniment for practice purposes; or to alter the piece to a more comfortable key. For maximum flexibility, you can purchase from MMO specialized CD players & recorders which allow variable speed while maintaining proper pitch, and vice versa. This is an indispensable tool for the serious musician and you may wish to look into purchasing this useful piece of equipment for full enjoyment of all your MMO editions.

We want to provide you with the most useful practice and performance accompaniments possible. If you have any suggestions for improving the MMO system, please feel free to contact us. You can reach us by e-mail at *info@musicminusone.com*.

3555

CONTENTS

©2011 MMO Music Group, Inc. All rights reserved.
ISBN 978-1-59615-789-7
1-59615-789-5

MMO 3555

French horn

Overture to Clementine

Ken Whitcomb

This arrangement copyright ©Ramapo Music.
All Rights Reserved. Used by Permission.

MMO 3555

Fascinating Rhythm

French horn

Words by Ira Gershwin
Music by George Gershwin
arr. Chas Warren

Copyright ©1924 WB MUSIC CORP. (Renewed)
This Arrangement Copyright ©2011 WB MUSIC CORP.
All Rights Reserved. Used by permission.

French horn

Music Man Medley

Meredith Willson
arr. Chas Warren

©1950, 1954, 1957, 1958 (Renewed) FRANK MUSIC CORP. and MEREDITH WILLSON MUSIC
This arrangement ©2011 FRANK MUSIC CORP. and MEREDITH WILLSON MUSIC
International Copyright Secured   All Rights Reserved.
Used by Permission

MMO 3555

MMO 3555

French horn

Funeral March of a Marionette

Charles Gonoud
adulterated by Chas Warren

©2007 Brasswagon Music www.chasmusic.com Used by permission,

A String of Pearls

French horn

by JERRY GRAY
arr. Chas Warren

Tempo di Mollusk ♩ = *160*

7 taps - 1 3/4 measures

©1941 (Renewed) CHAPPELL & CO., INC.
This Arrangement ©2011 CHAPPELL & CO., INC.
All Rights Reserved. Used by permission.

D. S. al Coda

Bocoxe

French horn

Baden Powell
arr. Buttery/Warren

Copyright © 2008 Cimarron Music Press. All rights reserved.
www.cimarronmusic.com Used by permission,

MMO 3555

Minnie the Moocher

French horn

Words & Music by
Cab Calloway & Irving Mills
arr. Chas Warren

©1932 EMI Mills Music Inc. and Gotham Music Service Inc.
This arrangement ©2011 EMI Mills Music Inc. and Gotham Music Service Inc. - Lawrence Wright Music Co. Ltd
All rights reserved. Used by permission,

Bist du bei mir

(IF THOU BE NEAR)

French horn

J. S. Bach
trans. Chas Warren

SOLO

Copyright © 2006 Cimarron Music Press. All rights reserved.
www.cimarronmusic.com Used by permission,

MMO 3555

Sabre Dance

French horn

Aram Khachaturian
arr. Paul Chauvin

©1987 Brasswagon Music. www.chasmusic.com
All rights reserved. Used by permission.

SAVAGE!!

MUSIC MINUS ONE
50 Executive Boulevard
Elmsford, New York 10523-1325
1.800.669.7464 (U.S.)/914.592.1188 (International)

www.musicminusone.com
e-mail: info@musicminusone.com